A PHOTOGRAPHIC JOURNEY

MEXICO

EXPLORAMA

MEXICO

MEXICO CITY

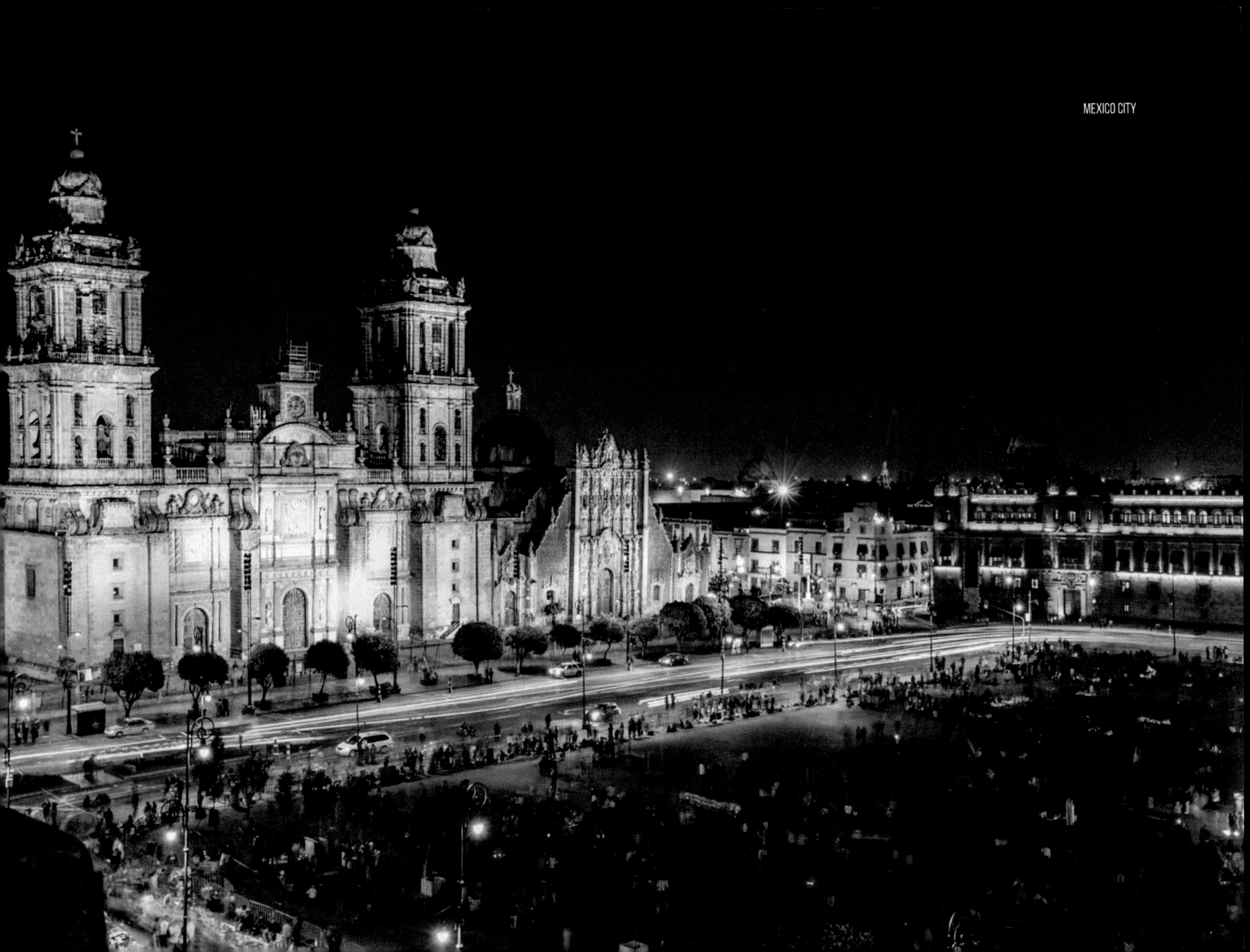

MEXICO CITY

MEXICO CITY

MEXICO CITY

MEXICO CITY

MEXICO CITY

MEXICO CITY

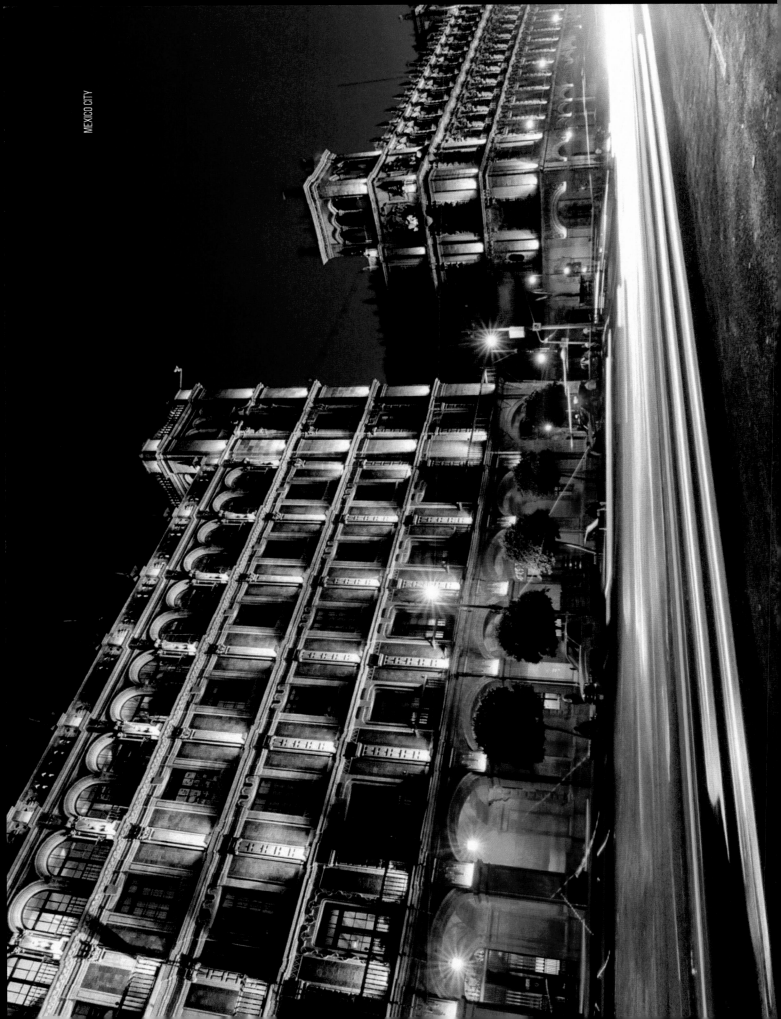

MEXICO CITY

MEXICO CITY

MEXICO CITY

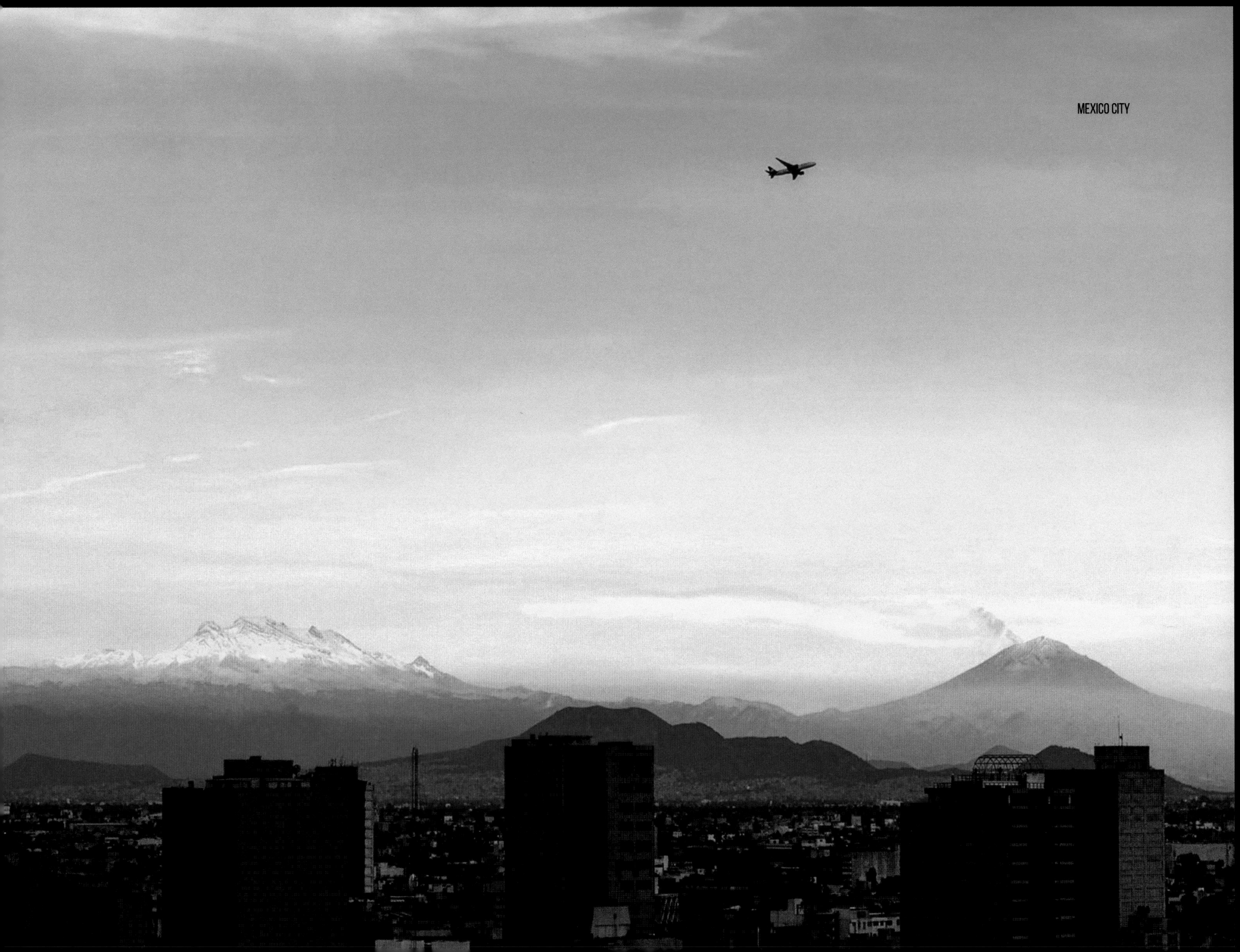

MEXICO CITY

MEXICO CITY

MEXICO CITY

MEXICO CITY

MEXICO CITY

CUETZALAN

CUETZALAN

TEOTIHUACÁN

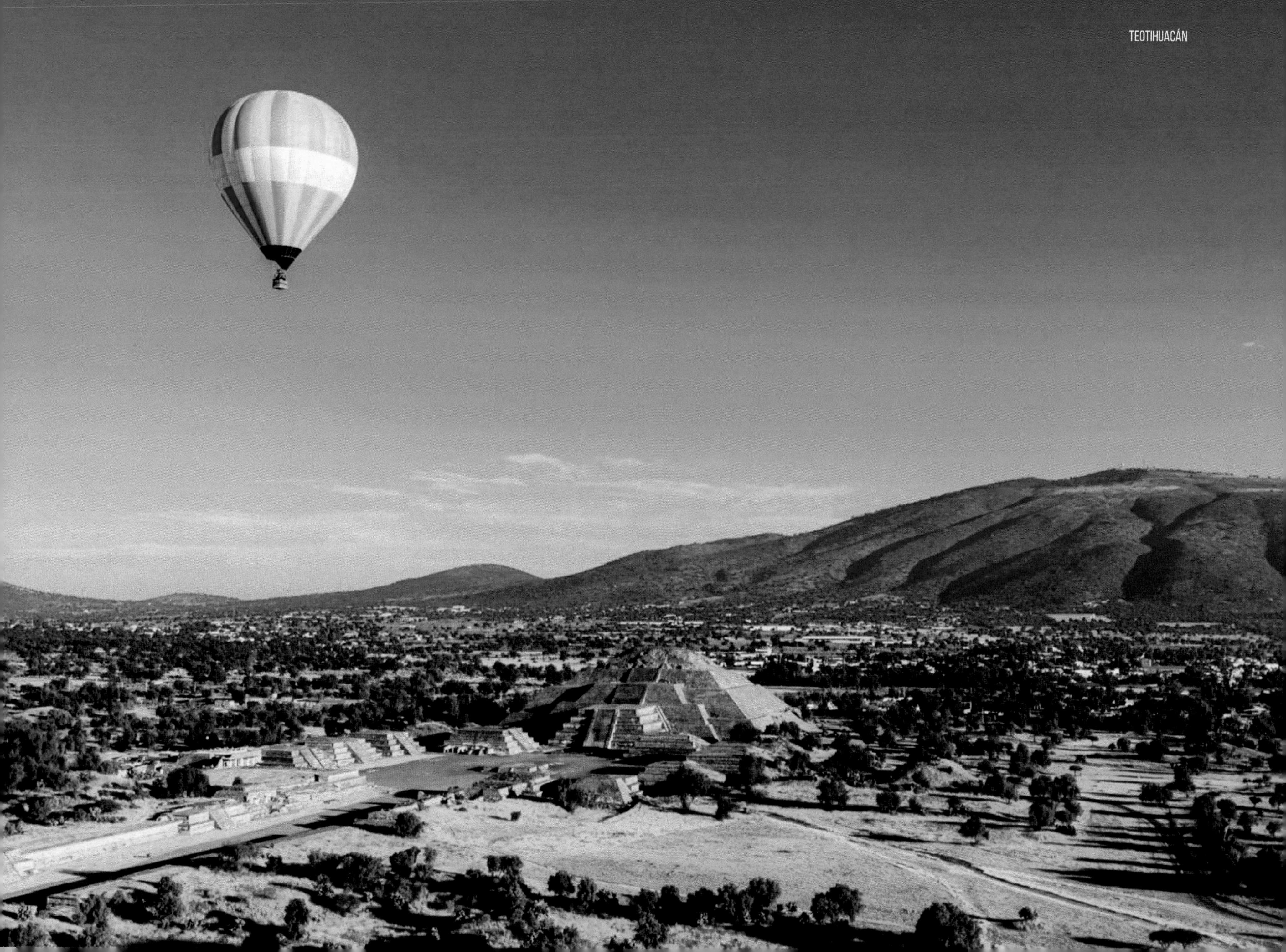

XOCHICALCO

TAXCO

TAXCO

TAXCO

TAXCO

TEPOTZOTLÁN

PUEBLA

PUEBLA

PUEBLA

PUEBLA

PUEBLA

LA MALINCHE

IZTACCÍHUATL

IZTACCÍHUATL

IZTACCIHUATL

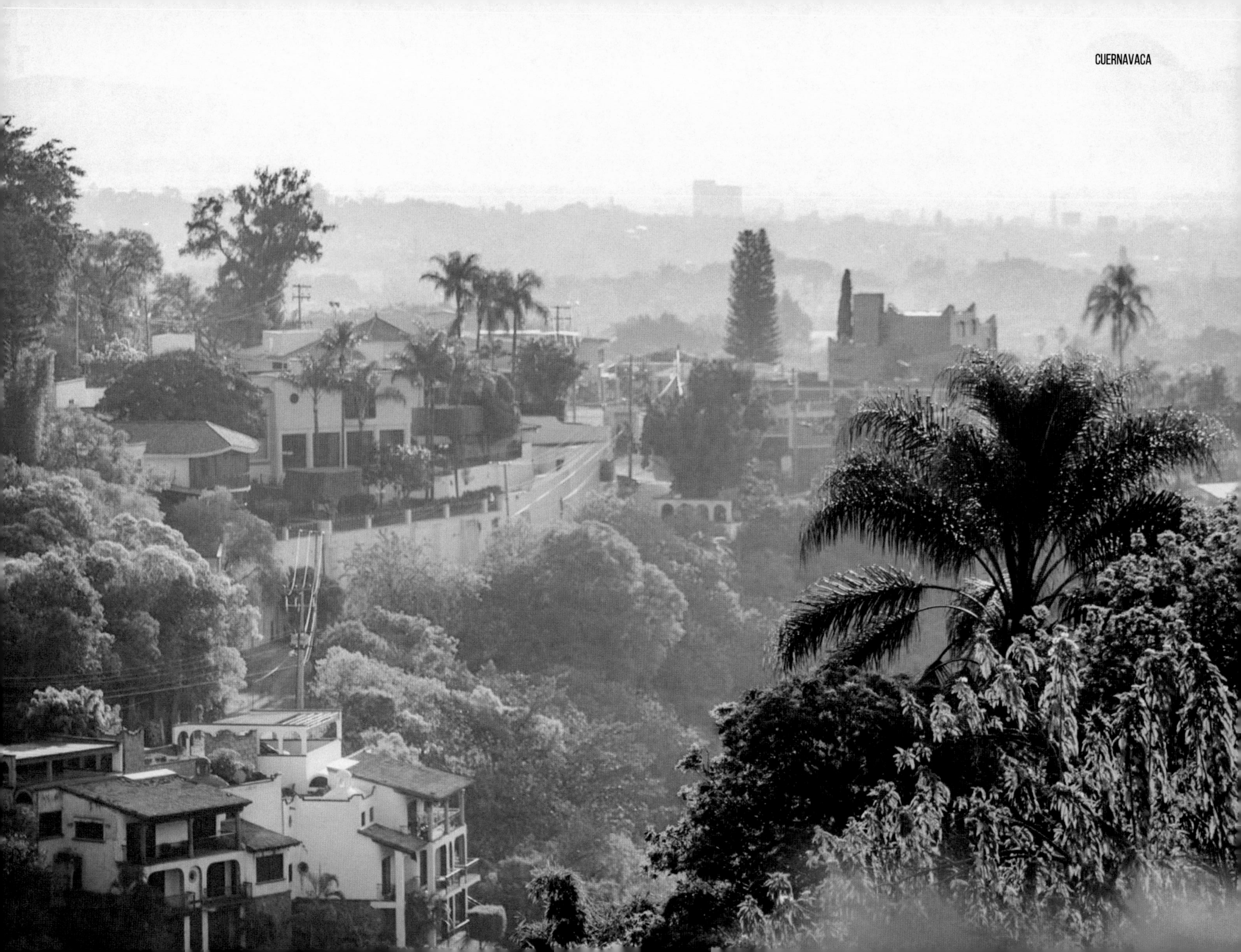
CUERNAVACA

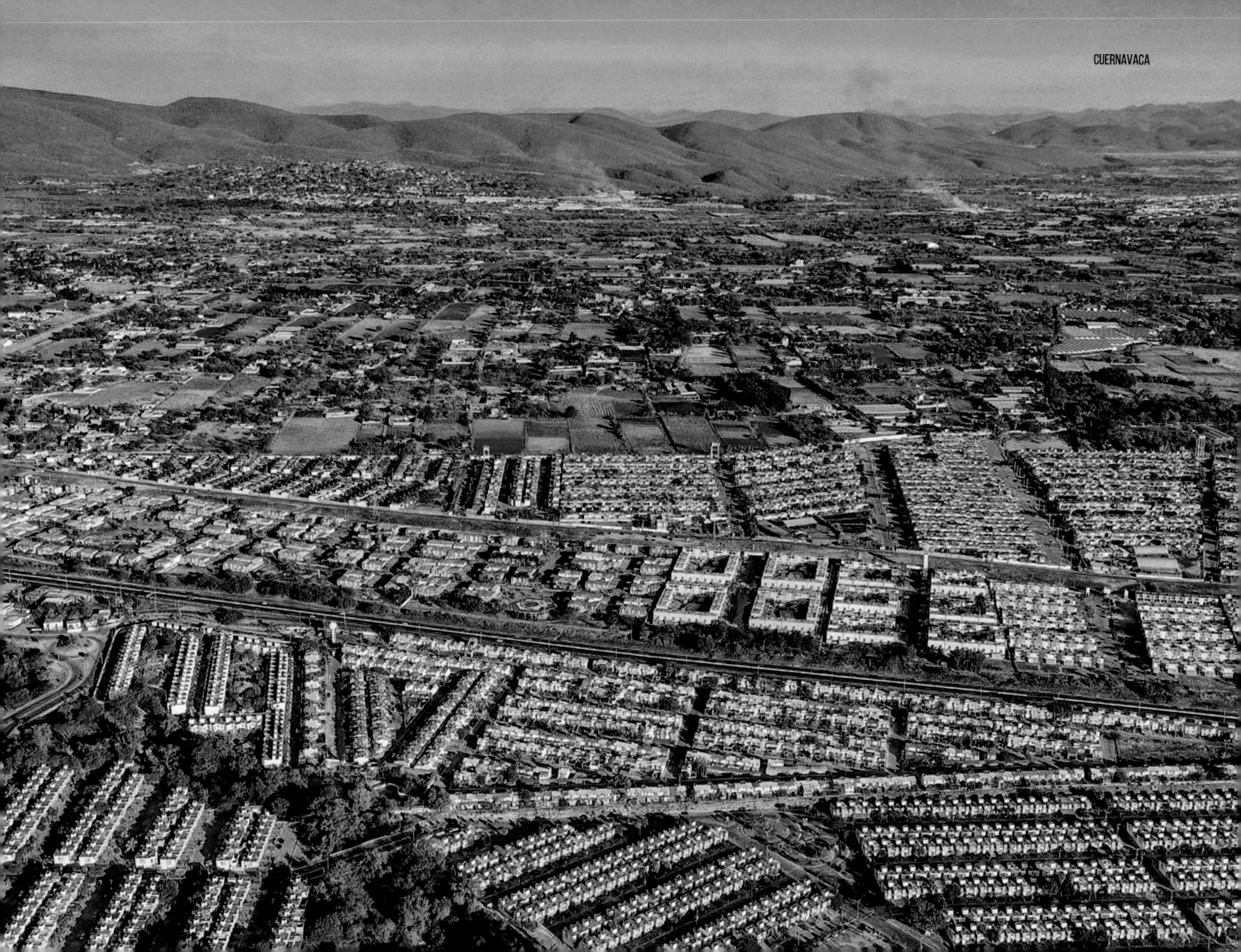
CUERNAVACA

VERACRUZ

TLACOTALPAN

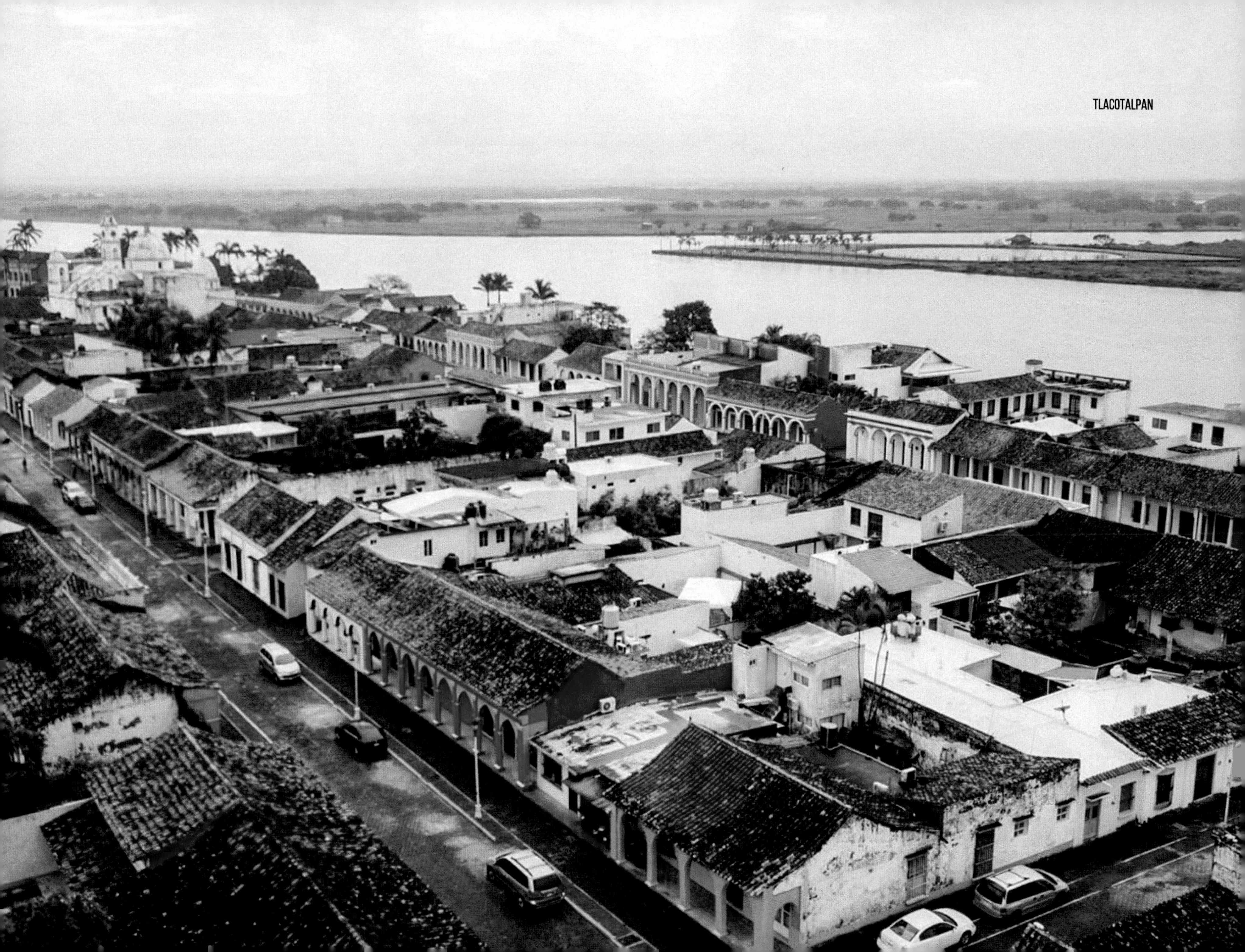
TLACOTALPAN

XALAPA

EL TAJÍN

EL TAJIN

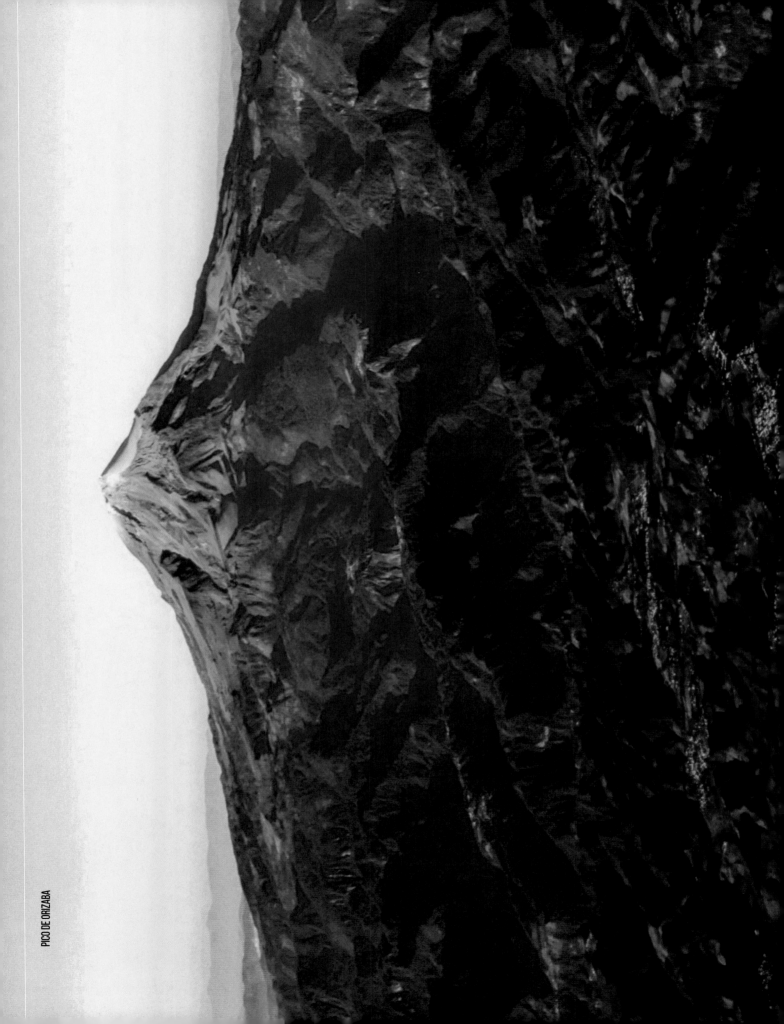

PICO DE ORIZABA

PICO DE ORIZABA

PAPANTLA

CANCUN

ISLA HOLBOX

ISLA HOLBOX

PUERTO MORELOS

PLAYA DEL CARMEN

ISLA COZUMEL

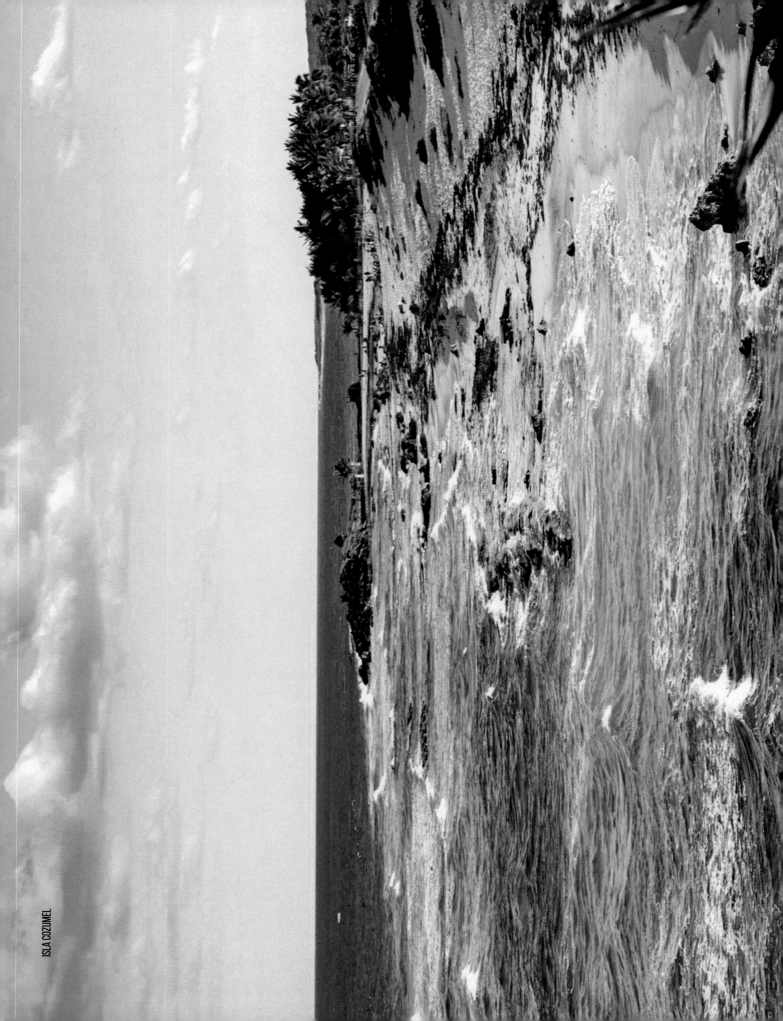

ISLA COZUMEL

MERIDA

MERIDA

DZIBILCHALTUN

IZAMAL

IZAMAL

CHICHEN ITZA

CHICHEN ITZA

CHICHEN ITZA

VALLADOLID

VALLADOLID

EK' BALAM

TULUM

TULUM

MAHAHUAL

MAHAHUAL

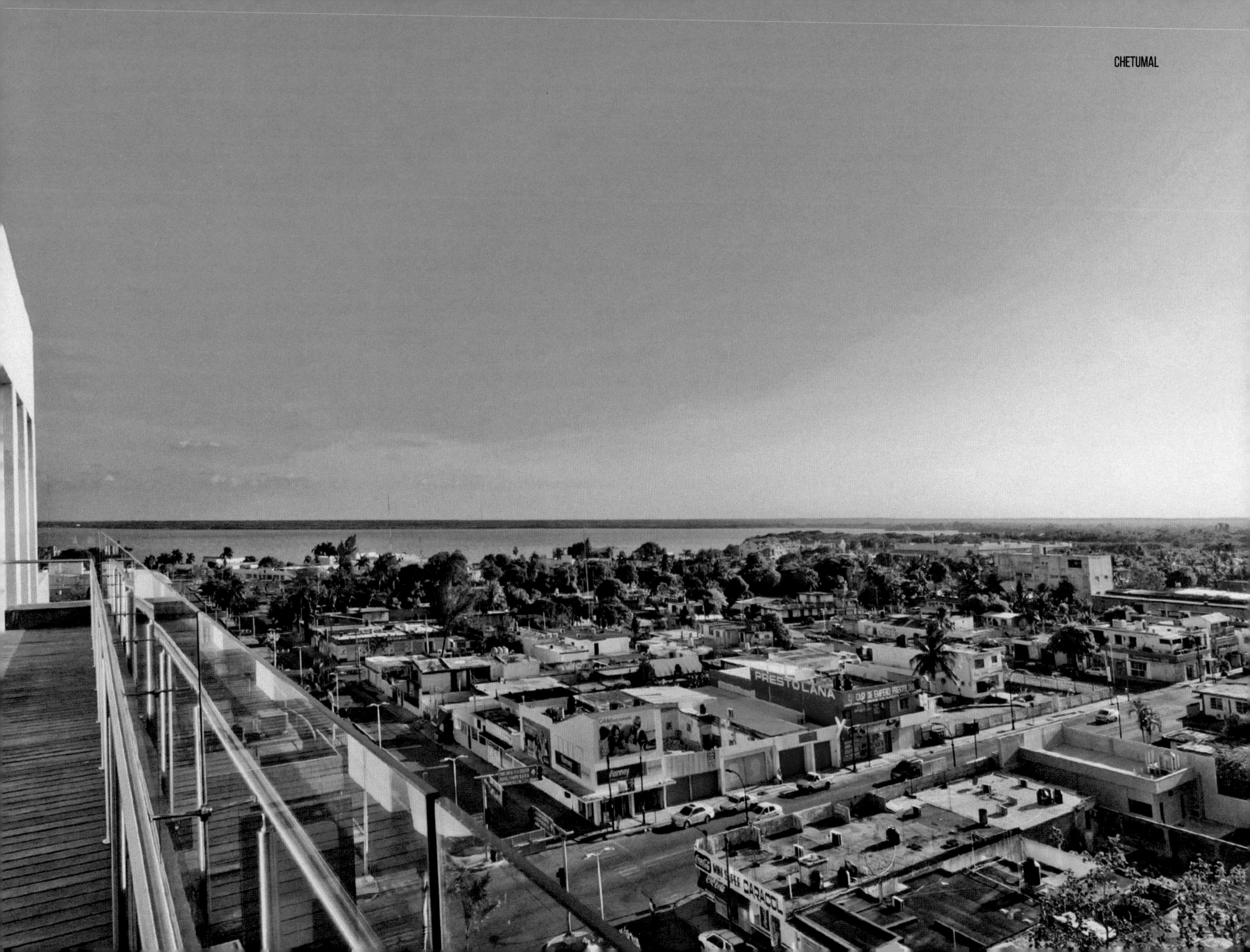
PRESTOLANA
CAJA DE EMPEÑO PRESTOLANA
CARACOL

CAMPECHE

XPUJIL

SAN CRISTÓBAL DE LAS CASAS

SAN CRISTÓBAL DE LAS CASAS

SAN CRISTÓBAL DE LAS CASAS

CAÑÓN DEL SUMIDERO

CAÑON DEL SUMIDERO

LAGUNA MIRAMAR

LACANDON JUNGLE

LAGOS DE MONTEBELLO

LAGOS DE MONTEBELLO

YAXCHILÁN

OAXACA CITY

OAXACA CITY

OAXACA CITY

MAZUNTE

ZIPOLITE

MONTE ALBÁN

MAZATLÁN

MAZATLÁN

PUERTO VALLARTA

PUERTO VALLARTA

ACAPULCO

ACAPULCO

SAYULITA

SAYULITA

ZIHUATANEJO

MORELIA

GUADALAJARA

GUADALAJARA

PATZCUARO

PARICUTÍN

VOLCÁN PARICUTÍN

TEQUILA

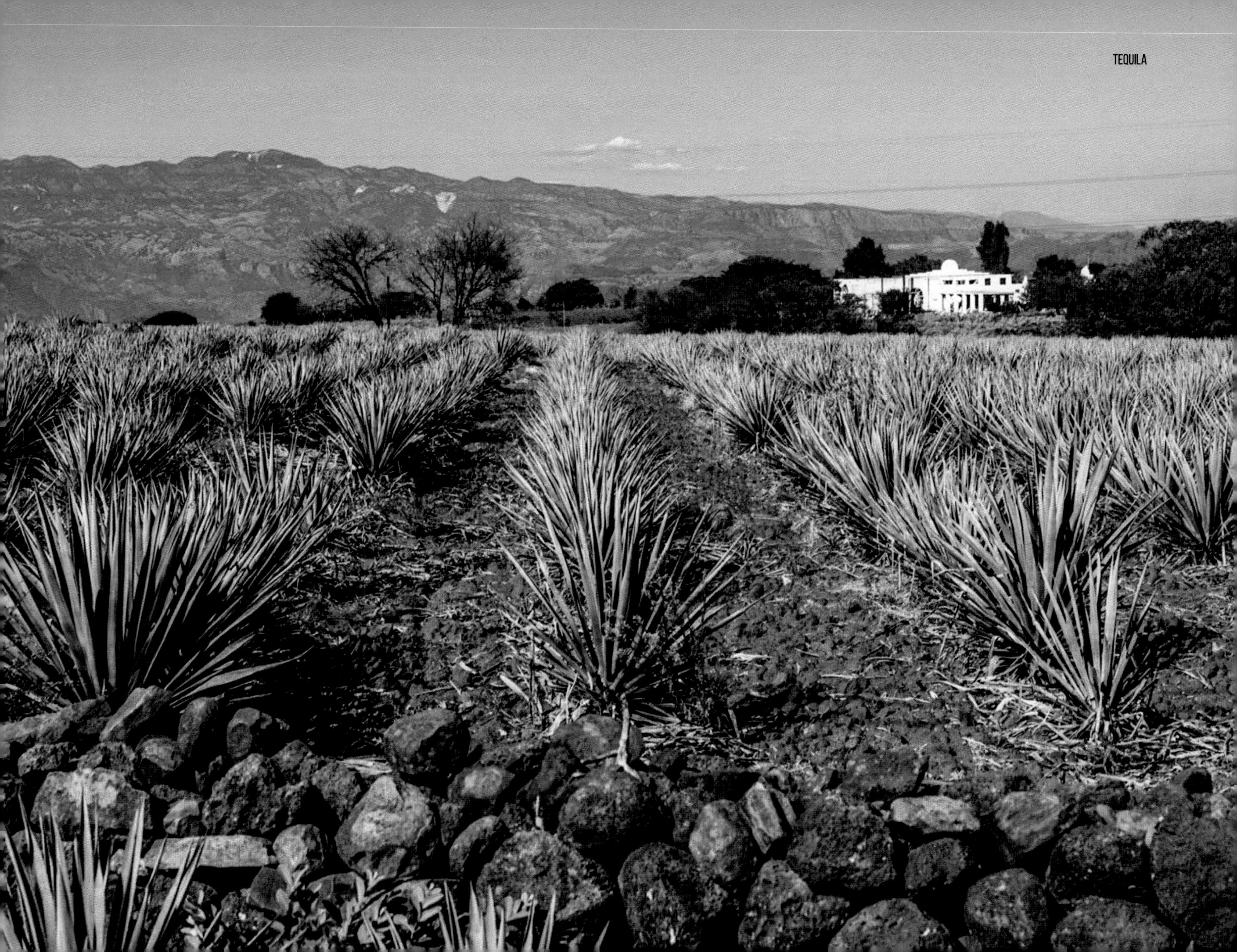

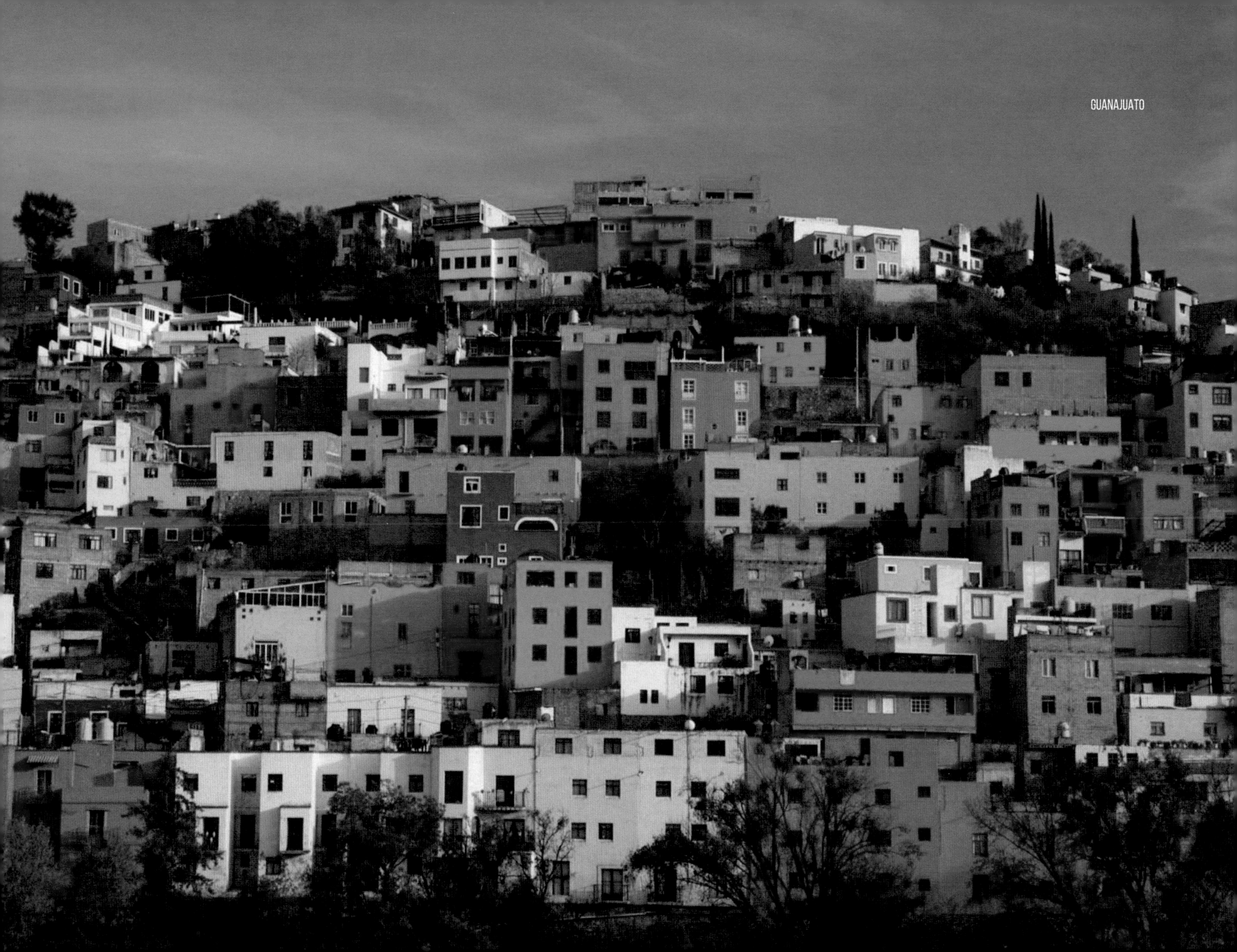

GUANAJUATO

GUANAJUATO

SAN MIGUEL DE ALLENDE

SAN MIGUEL DE ALLENDE

SAN MIGUEL DE ALLENDE

SIERRA GORDA

HUASTECA POTOSINA

AGUASCALIENTES

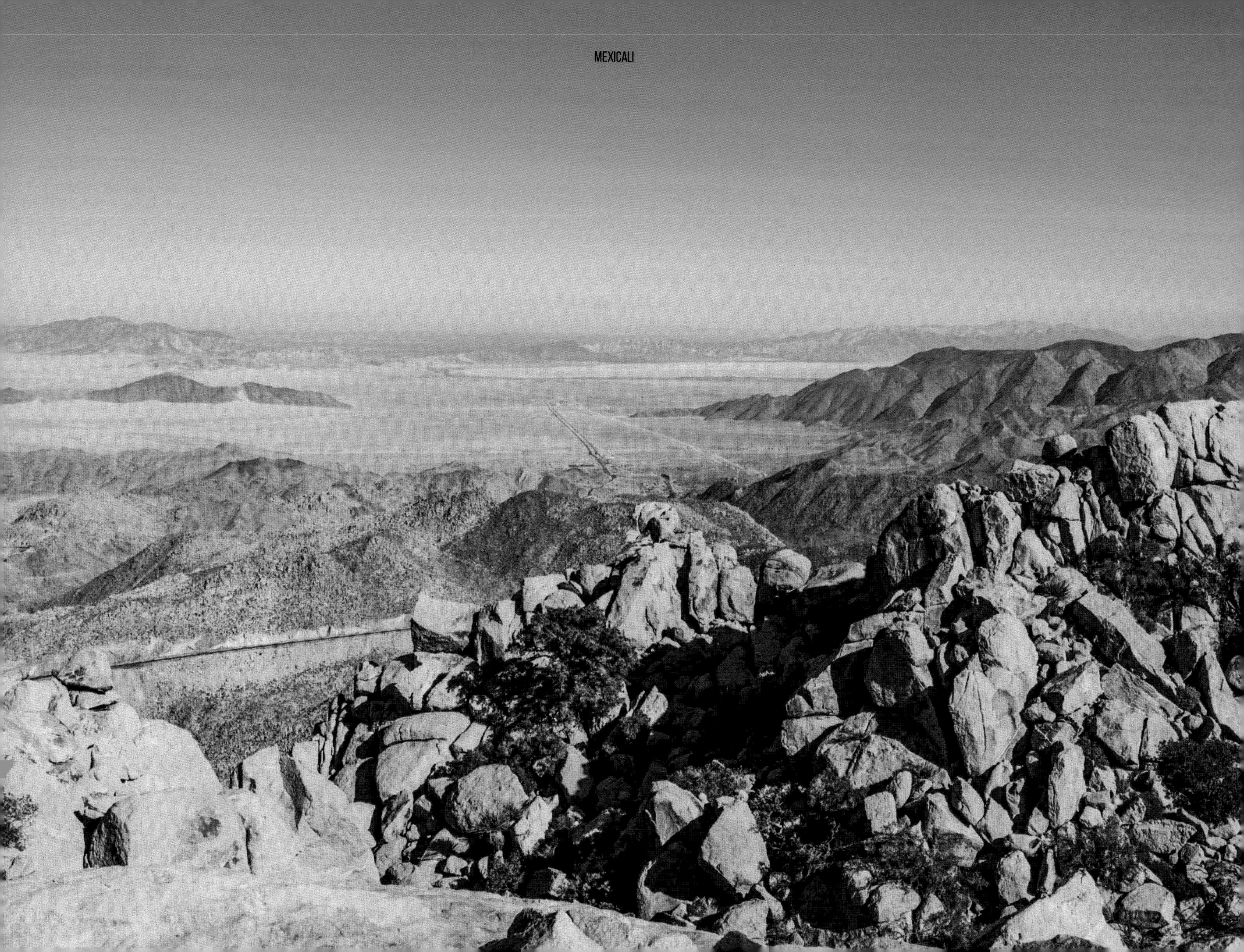
MEXICALI

VALLE DE GUADALUPE

LORETO

CABO SAN LUCAS

CABO SAN LUCAS

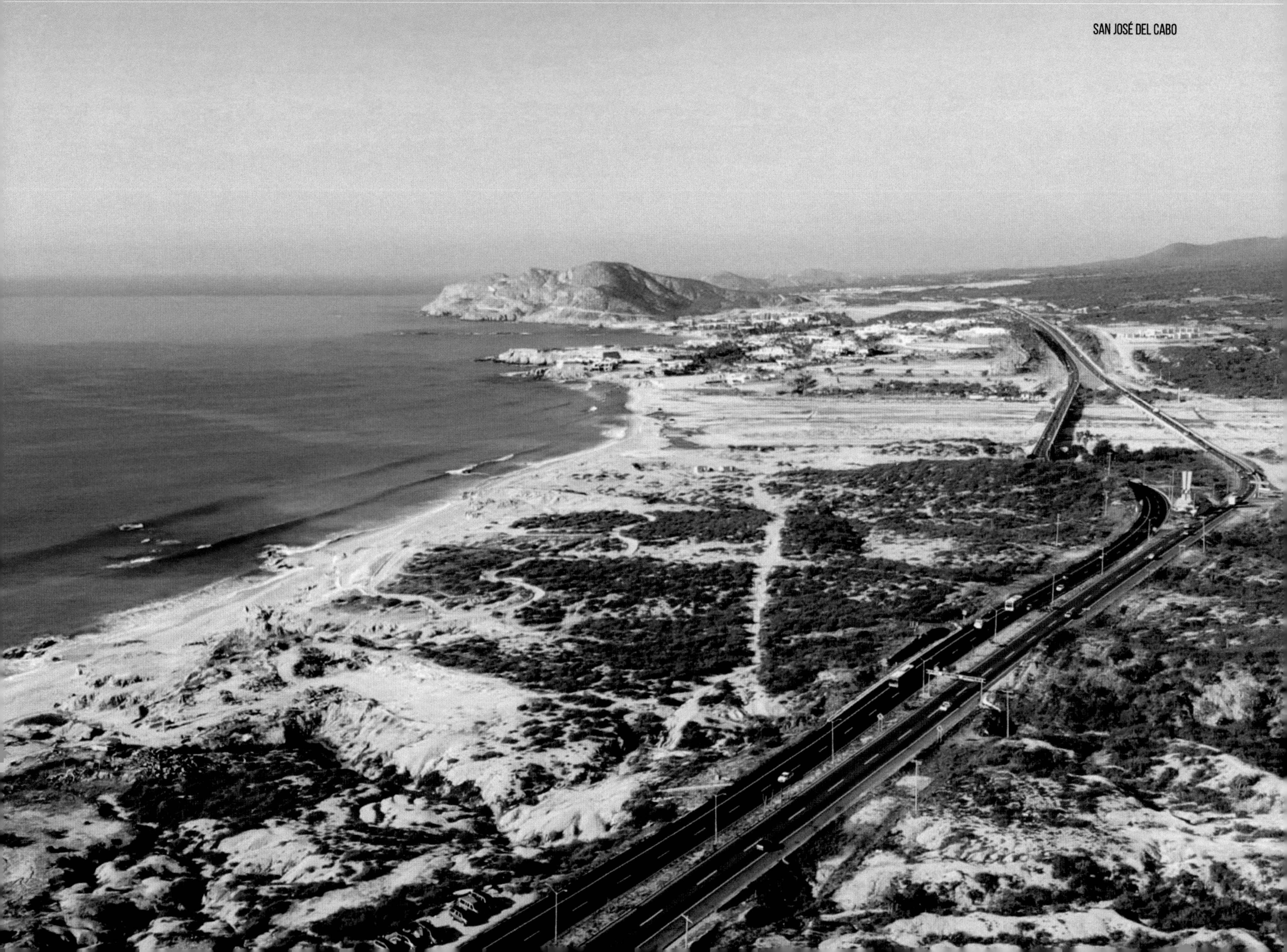

SAN JOSÉ DEL CABO

SAN JOSÉ DEL CABO

LA PAZ

MONTERREY

SIERRA MADRE

SIERRA MADRE

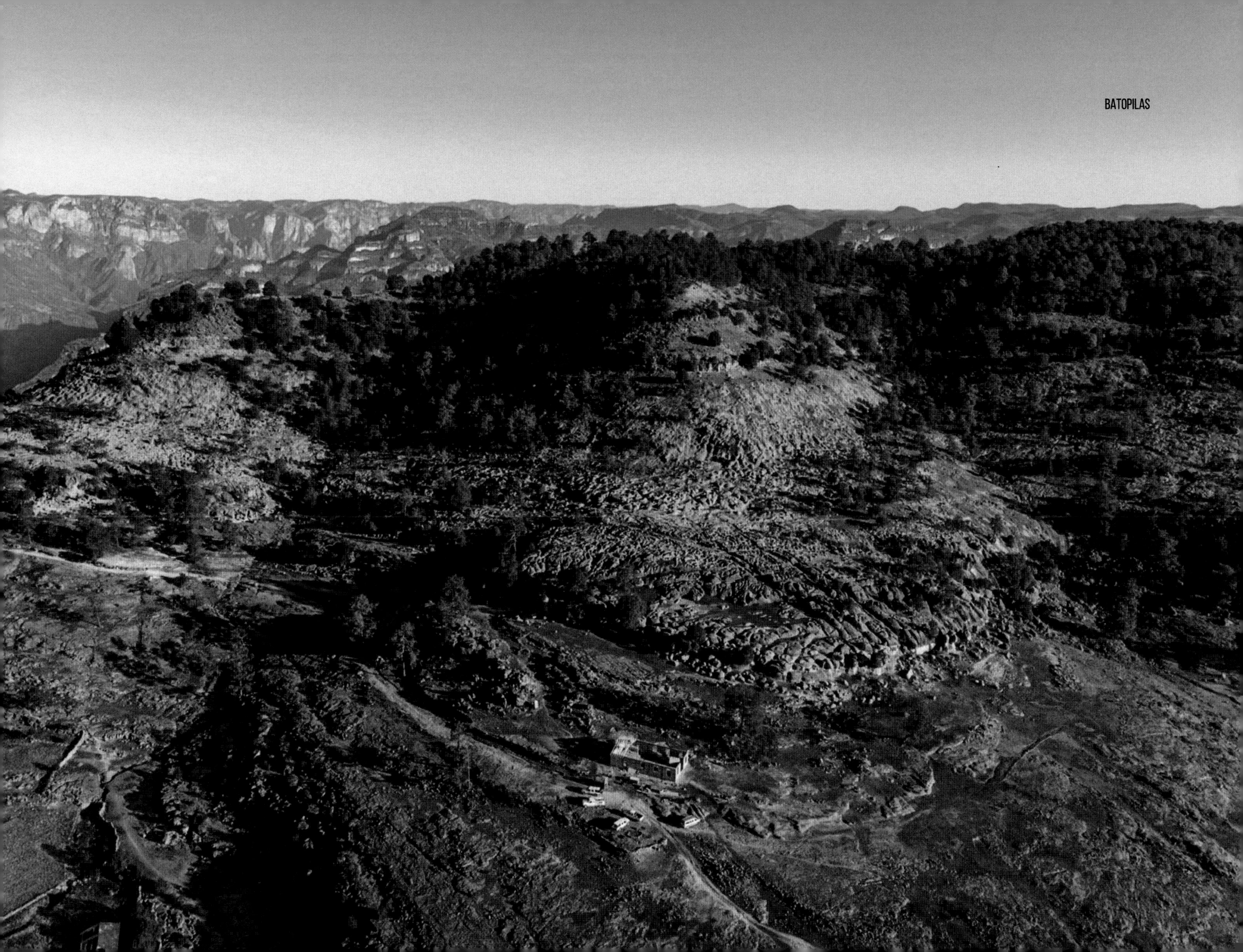
BATOPILAS

CASCADA DE BASASEACHI

MEXICO

Explorama

Made in the USA
Las Vegas, NV
08 December 2024

13644282R00112